hangover days

to trystan - for being my best friend, my muse, my conscience, my wife, and far too often, my caretaker

and to my parents - for this life (no matter how much i bitch about it)
and to gene - for being my brhanother, my confidant, and work-for-free editor
and to the friends who keep me artistic and drink on my front porch until two am on weeknights

Table of Contents

baby on baby	7
twenty-six, married	10
eight days a week	12
I'm sorry for myself	14
diamonds and rust	16
You are getting Greedy.	17
CASINO	19
Bourdain's cameraman	21
this is what love looks like	23
enough with the questions	26
Somerdale news and tobacco	28
252mi to empty	29
they don't teach you that in school	31
two dreams in the same night involving the same characters, or one long dream	33
over a year	36
Paterson, N.J.	38
scam of life	40
the ____ remains the same	41
t-9hrs	42
pretend	45
one new image	46
memoir	48
intelligence	50
cold water	51
getting close	54
couch (the worst last name)	58
Fortune cookie	60
Bourdain	63
chupacabra	64
heel turn	65
closer.	67
number five	69
there's no beauty in sanity	70
ayatollah	71
BMW	73
did I get too fat?	75
at the airport	77
checkmate	78
hangover days	79

mean girls	82
idols	84
rebound	86
the bandaid	87
triple j	89
the dog deserves better	90
lie, lie, lie	92
blue-balls	94
Omega	96
Nathaniel	99
hide	101
models	103
Bag of Scum	105
a cliche, positive poem	106
making his way to the ring…	107
happy with that	109
sacrifices.	111
next	114
the blowjob mystery	115
the piano movers	117
ode to fucking	120
sober	121
I didn't eat lunch yet	122
deerskin	124
coco	126
you sounded good	128
start writing	130
steel-toe	131
afraid	133
a fly in the mansion	135
2020	138
judgement-free	141
striped shirts and mini skirts	142
the reason(?)	143
capitol hill	145
Takotsubo	147
thursday in december	150
the death of Dick Clark	153
inside a barn-like house	154
one more	156
worthless	158
pimples	160
wine and cheese	162

green vests	163
that simple	165
Jameson	166
history	168
magnanimous	169
just one	170
w-r-r-i-i-g-t-h-e-t	171
two day withdrawal	172
un cafè	174
Trophy	175
tomorrow	176
These Family Parties	178
the days run wild…	180
Wisdom	183
the poems that talk about struggle	185
the new place	186
and I stare at her	187
The Jazz Age	189
sunday morning poems	190
The Burden of the Mind	192
salt.	193
Postcard from North Adams, MA	194
Return Postcard from North Adams, MA	196
Petting Zoo on Lower Landing Rd	197
Oh, Artie!	198
one for two	200
Note to Self	202
the herd	203
non-refundable	204
Mr. Knuckles	205
Lumos	206
light of life, black of death	208
Last Will and Testicle	210
how it's supposed to be	212
hands of a god	213
Ding, Ding, Ding	214
greener	215
inspiration without adaptation	216
death of a salesman	217
brachium	218
both	220
better than you	221
ballet	222

Inner Child	223
a spider	224
60 degrees	225
a book you still hide	226
Power	228
4am	229
#002	230
1,715 ft.	231
16th and Locust	233
I	234
3/26/22	238
Scottsville, Virginia	239
Born too late	241
24 hours	242
a conversation on a park bench	234
full time	245
Hemingway's Challenge Pt.2	246
Hemingway's Challenge Pt.5	247
watching the game at a brewery	248
"K"	249
new york, new york	250
evolution: 1	252
glee	254
My Masterpiece	255

baby on baby

"

you haven't painted
in four years
and
you only read
because you think
you have to
and because
other people do
and you're only
writing
because you're
rereading
all the shit
you have before
just to say
you're a reader
and you
stopped drumming
three years ago
yet always
talk about how
you were a
musician
and you stopped
acting when it
got hard
instead of practicing
how to talk
but oh
you're a writer
you're a poet
so you don't have
to talk
you're a drummer
so you don't have
to talk
you're a painter
so you don't have
to talk
but

for someone
who doesn't want
to talk
you sure as hell
talk constantly
about how great
of an artist
you are
and how much
artistic shit
you have done
in such a short life
and look
at all the lives
you've already lived
you're so talented
but
you haven't
done a goddamn
thing in years
you fucking bum
because
you have no idea
who you are
do you
because whatever
you read or watch
or listen to is now
your personality
because you
don't have your own
and
that is why
you've done so much
because you've quit
so much
and
don't stick to
anything
so no
you are not
an artist
and sure

you used to be
but
you aren't now
                    "

i look at her
and say

"this is why I married you"

twenty-six, married

can't stop at
                one

the two of us
walk into
what a google search
shows to be the
closest
and perhaps
best?
dive bar
that is on our way home

there is a twenty-seven foot
nineteen-eighties bar
that wraps around
the entire building
like a biblical snake

out of the fifty-six seats
only five are taken
and they are split
by two identical-
looking bald guys
in union garb
that must have had
an early day of going
down manholes
and
three men
above sixty -
only one,
again,
with hair

the one with hair
is shouting his
life story -
particularly last nights -
where he was *this* close
to having that threesome

and *hey, man, you can ask*
the bartender, man, she was
here last night

the bartender ignores him
as she comes to us
and asks what we would like

two modelos,
order of wings

what time is it?

three fifteen

what time does your
wife need you home

five thirty, you?

about then

alright,
we will leave at
four forty-five

eight days a week

oops,
i did it again

beers at work
caused a text
to friends
to continue
drinking after work

on a tuesday

and those beers
after the first beers
caused beers
to happen at
their house
until 11:30

on a tuesday

the beers
after the first beers
after the second beers
caused me to think
i was an artist
and belittle
the real artists
that you like
and
you didn't need
all those beers
to tell me
i was a fake artist
and an asshole

on a tuesday

you sleep downstairs
and i sleep alone
and wake up hungover
and alone

and miss work

on a wednesday

and get so depressed
that i had
those beers

on a tuesday

and i send my
apology texts
that i just
copy and paste
whenever i do this

on a monday
on a tuesday
on a wednesday
on a thursday
on a friday
on a saturday
on a sunday

i'm sorry for myself

it's always after
drinking

that the voice
comes back
in
like a
breeze on
a farm
like
Ricky Ricardo

and he says
you are despicable
you are embarrassing
you are a joke

and you scream back
I KNOW
I KNOW
I KNOW

and you chain
smoke
outside until
the spins stop
and
you look through
the window
at your wife
moving her pillow
to the couch
and
you look down
and close your eyes
and plan your suicide
tomorrow
after
you apologize
to everyone

and you
stumble to bed
alone
and sad
and you
were doing so well
so well
so well
oh well
tomorrow is
already ruined

everything is ruined

diamonds and rust

give me
a hotel room

please

i always sleep
the best
in
a hotel room

no cats
no dogs
no lights
no snoring
no memories
no permanence

just the comfort
of a foreign place
with the view
of the same world

You are getting Greedy.

i don't see the world
in colors anymore

my face has aged
more in four years
than obama's did

my voice has changed
my body has changed
my mindset has changed
my humor has changed

my hands are not mine
my eyes are not mine
my nose is not mine
my heart is not mine
my possessions are not
mine

i own nothing
i have become nothing

no passions
no happiness
no goal
no love
no energy
no will

humans do not make me
happy
loneliness does not make me
happy
i do not make me
happy

i am waiting for it
all
to change
without the
work

work
work
work
work

work

i forget how to eat
i forget how to walk
i forget how to talk
i forget how to fuck
i forget how to love

i forget me
i forget me
i forget me
i forget
me
me
me

me

burn out.

CASINO

"you just hit this button
to bet the minimum
or this button
to bet the max."
i said to her
"and this is the most
important
button of them all,"
i continued
"the cocktail button.
you press this and
a waitress
who grandmothers
sixty-seven and smokes
more than me
comes out and gives you a
cocktail or beer
or whatever the fuck
for free."

"should we tip them
a dollar?"
she asked

"yeah, fine,
tip them a dollar."

the casino
is a beautiful place

the food is great, now
and the sounds
the smell of cigars
smoked and chewed on
the free booze
(as long as you're winning)
and the guarantee of
sex

win or lose
it's the one thing

the house can't take
away

Bourdain's cameraman

"I'm not happy,
I'm doing well,
much better than
I was,
but I am not happy."

he told me.

I let it hang there
and took a sip
and asked him

"how can that be true
when you are famous
and successful -

how can you be doing
well
and not be happy"

"I am not successful",
he told me,
"you are successful.
you are happy.
you said yourself
you are happy
with your fiancée

and that is the difference."

I looked at his finger
empty
I looked at his eyes
empty
I looked at his glass
empty

I got us two more
beers

"so you have the money

                    the career"
I asked him,
"but not the girl?"

"yes"
he said,
"yes, I don't have
the girl"

"you are living my dream
making money as an
artist
and seeing the world

but
like bourdain
like the rest
you need the girl"

"yes"
he said,
"yes, I don't have
the girl

and you are successful."

this is what love looks like

lips together,
    then separate
and as you come away
she smiles
shyly,
bites her lip,
looks up at you,
and you do it again
and again

and her hand
presses
the back of your head
closer
and your hair
surfaces in between
her fingers

and you reach under
and
squeeze her ass
slide your fingers
down
and in -
and you keep kissing her,
her neck now
and feel her
more wet
more ready

and her hand
finds you
and strokes
up
  and
    down
   up
  and
    down

your legs and feet

kick off remaining
        clothes
and you roll on top
squeeze her chest
slide it in
look into eyes
        soul
          pulse
    and pulse
    and pulse

and she grabs your arm
kisses it
grabs it tighter
digs in

sound comes and goes
      comes and goes

you kiss in stride
her nails scratch
your back
your shoulder
your chest

she rolls you over
kisses your neck
      your chest
      your hip
and she tastes you
like it's the last time
chokes on you
then slides you in

she pins your arms down
takes control
you are hers
and she is free
to use you
to love you
to be herself

your bodies covered

in blood
and saliva
and sweat

and you both tense
and release
and collapse

in-to each other

and you hold her
and forget about work
          and money
          and friends
          and family
          and your car
          and your coffee
          and your extra fat
          and your credit score
          and your enemies
          and your anxiety

and you realize
this is what love looks like

enough with the questions

a third?

yes

you got a third dui?

yes

are you joking?

no

you know there are
ubers right?

yes

so what the hell?

answer that yourself

what?

answer that yourself

what do you mean?

think about it

what do you mean?

i mean
if i could think clearly
a lot more
would be different

but no one stopped you?

no

why?

because only care
about themselves

are you going
to rehab now?

no

are you going to
prison?

maybe

don't you love me?

yes

are you sure?

yes

so why would you
keep doing this to me?

i don't know

should i leave you?

probably

aren't you going
to fight?

i don't know

when will this end?

Somerdale news and tobacco

he asked for a quick six
a five pick
a powerball ticket
three quick pick fours
and another quick six
then he turned
and looked at me
and turned back around
and asked for
another powerball
another five
two more six picks
and two scratch-offs
then he dug into his overalls
and found a quarter
and played the scratch-offs
and won two bucks
and asked for
another powerball
then he took
his wallet out
and emptied it
onto the counter
and four dollars
and three quarters
came out
and he asked for
two more fives
and one more six
and then he left

then I walked up
and asked for cigarettes

252mi to empty

I actually like this
         job
I swear to god
        I do,

love it, maybe
and
I complain, yes
of course,
but not like I did before

,but   ,
you see,

I'm sitting in my car
writing
and shaking
and
thinking about creating
a mural
with my thoughts
and brains
and failures

because I have
         two hours
left before I can leave
without confrontation
and
they want me to work
with three strangers

why can't I do that?
         //
why do I still have these
attacks
on my body and mind?
         //

they were to leave
when I found a job

I liked deep down
 deep deep down

but they remain,
like a song you hate,
like a comma

is it from time
holding me prisoner,
using verbal batons
or
am I still afraid
of strangers

like a moth
to a dragonfly,
I stay in my car
and wait
to be fired

they don't teach you that in school

you have a history
of not keeping jobs,

but that is not your fault -
there is always something
                better
and you get bored
easily

you like the finer things
because you visualize
confidence -

no one in the crackhouse
is happy

the fat mailman
makes more than you
and gets three times
the pussy -

he likes the common
and the simple,

it is not because
he looks better than
you
or works harder
or is less fucked up

he works
without stress because
he is too dumb
to stress

he lives in a house
with broken doors
and broken bottles

he does not wish
to be in the top

percent
unless it is handed to him

you do

so work means something
    work means nothing
it is a means to fund
your passion(s)

a career is for social security
and that will not exist
by the time you can get it
anyway

you will never have enough
money,
no matter your taste
or lifestyle

pussy can be bought
and so can the lottery

those with mansions
are never home
to see them

you can work at Walmart
and own a BMW,
you just have to live
out of it

you can never have it all
you must always sacrifice
something that you love
for something else
        that you love

and they don't teach you
balance
in school

**two dreams in the same night
involving the same characters,
or one long dream**

I

I looked out my window
into my backyard
one spring day

and
found
my two dogs
and a new, strange white dog
staring into the neighbor's yard

and in his yard
was his dog
and
then the new white dog
ran into the fence
and started destroying it
desperately trying to attack
the neighbor's dog

my two dogs cowered
and ran into their doghouse
while the white dog
broke piece by piece
off the wooden fence

my neighbor came out
old, grey-haired, and prickish
and yelled at me
about the white dog

I told him
I had no idea where it came from
or who it belonged to
and the neighbor cursed
and went back inside

I was confused about

his lack of concern
as the white dog
broke through the fence

I called my wife frantically
while she was at work
and begged her
to come home

and when she did
she calmly said
that the white dog
was hers
and that there was
nothing to worry about

the white dog was now family

II

the old neighbor
kept speaking to my wife
as the days passed
and they got very
friendly

so friendly that even
other people would comment
on it
and I would laugh it off
saying it's harmless
since their age difference
was so spectacular

like Deb and Lundy
I would say
forgetting that they dated

and one day
I was in the yard
(the white dog was gone)
and my wife
came outside

and told me the neighbor
wanted money for something
I forget what
maybe to fix the fence

and she smiled
in a way that
sex makes you smile
in a way that
made you
want to kill her
so I pinned her to
the ground
and asked what he wanted
and she said $400
and I said no
fuck him
and she pleaded with me
so I pinned her down more
and asked if she gave him
the money yet
and she said no
and I said are you sure
and she said no
and I screamed
HOW COULD YOU

III

and
beep beep beep
it was 8:30
and my wife and I
woke up and got ready
for work

over a year

it's been over
          a year
since I've written
a
  single
 poem

it's been over
          a year
since I started
working
  with the
 devil

I made
my vice
my career

since this one
isn't working
        out

and neither am I

and I blame
my new career
because
I don't just
drink the beer
now
I make it

I found what I love
and
it's killing me

I gained 50 lbs
and make no art
and sleep too much
and eat all carbs
and drive only drunk

and my luck
will run out soon

which is not
good -
especially when you're
25.

Paterson, N.J.

in the parking lot
of a Salvation Army
there are
three
Mercedes-Benz
and
two Audi

and
a guy walks
out of the building
with his jacket
bunched and he is
hunched
and pants fall
from under his jacket
and he proclaims
"I AIN'T
 STEAL
  NOTHIN'"

and
I walk
around the building
and a junkie
walks into the woods
topless with
dirt on her breasts
and her nipples
pointing to the sun

and she washes
a shirt
in a bucket
of rain water
and is joined
by a man
weighing sixty pounds
who washes his body
with the same bucket
and same rain water

and
I walk back
around the building
and
through a fence
I see a young man,
nearly still a kid,
sitting on a ledge
that is over
the Passaic River
and he sticks a needle
in his arm
and puts his head back
and his eyes close
and he nods
and he sways
and he falls
fifty feet into
the river -
his backpack
still on the ledge

and I walk
north
trying to escape
and at the border
of Paterson,
right at the edge,
right where it ends,
there is a waterfall
and it is beautiful
and I stare at it

and I hope we never
work here again

scam of life

the main difference
is

when you are
a child

having fun
is
free

when you are
an adult

having fun
is
expensive

as is freedom
as is sex
as is death

and they don't
even
pay you
for suicide

the ____ remains the same

you
have so many problems
and conflicts
that you can't solve

you
need a new place to live
or your marriage
will fall apart
but she makes more
than you
but your credit is better

you
need to move
but the problems
remain
the same

you
need a car
but
see above

you
think about
all the solutions
that are too far
to grab
so

you
grab her
and kiss her neck
and pull her ass in
and fuck her

because
it is the only thing
you can do

t-9hrs

at 8:15am
I decided that
after work   I would
get in my car
and drive

    to Virginia
    or Vermont

no text
no call
no note

I would stop
at the bank
    withdraw
my petty cash
and put it in the trunk
for her to find

I would drive
and   drive
and get to 105mph
and turn left   sharply
into the barricade

at 8:20am
I decided that
I should write a note
on break

at 8:21am
I decided that
I won't

at 8:30am
I decided that
my vision was hindering
my job performance
and the blurry view
and mental clock

was being noticed

at 8:33am
I decided that
I will change
the podcast
I was listening to
from talking to music
back to talking
back to music
in an effort
to be more productive

at 8:34am
I decided that
I will listen
to nothing

at 8:40am
I decided that
if my wife
called me
while I was driving
I would answer
to hear her voice
one last time

at 8:41am
I decided that
the conversation
would go as follows:
"hey where are you?
why are you not home yet?
-
"hi baby. I love you.
I'm sorry. this wasn't
something you could
control."
-
"Robbie wha-"
click.

at 8:42am

I decided that
having tears streaming
down my face
at work
was the reason
my boss was walking
over to me

at 8:43am
I decided that
I would tell him
that I just couldn't
stop yawning

at 8:44am
I decided that
her voice and face
would not leave my mind

at 8:45am
I decided that
I drive home today
after work

at 8:46am
I decided that
I would not
cancel my plans
the next time
they entered my
mind

at 8:47am
I decided that
I would never
buy a gun

at 8:48am
I decided that
I would go back
to therapy

pretend

I've found
that there is no
money
in poetry
or art

so I find new
hobbies
and call them
passions

and I get invested
and learn all I can
and they last a few
months

then I try another
and every time
I do this
I forget about
poetry
or art
for a little while

but I always come back
and it is always
like finding it again
for the first time

if only I could
pay the bills

I could stop
pretending

one new image

my phone
lights up across
    the room
as I read Bukowski
on the couch

and it says
"one new image"
and instead of
thinking nothing
or something
better
I think
"it's my wife
sending me a picture
of herself
naked
in bed
with another man"

it's unfair,
really,
how I can't read
in peace
without my mind
filling my thoughts
and vision
with nausea
and
making me write
these sad sad poems
instead of letting
me be happy
or even content

the world is not
out to get
me

I'm
out to get

me

and
I've got
me

memoir

in bed
and my eyes keep closing
but I cannot sleep

so I write
this poem
this memoir
for you in the morning

in bed
and I look at the ceiling
with two water streaks

parallel
nevermore
like that song
or our foreign lives

in bed
and I think about
if I should have fucked

all those girls
no
you would not have
liked that

in bed
and our ankles
are swollen

from the walks
closer
then further apart
from Vermont

in bed
and I'm typing
too loud

and I woke you

up again
for another
bad poem

intelligence

she loved my
intelligence
more than anything,

but she always spelled
"intelligence"
wrong

cold water

the bath is now cold
like iceland
or greenland?
like my arrogance
and laziness

she gets home
in an hour
and
I've been sitting
in this water
for two hours
and
have two hours
worth of errands
to do
and
I promised her
I would clean
the house
she pays for
but
I stay
in the cold water
and write
about my arrogance
and laziness

as if she will
never leave me

or stop
fucking me
even   though
the two hours
I've been in
the cold water
has accomplished
one and a half hours
of porn
and two

climaxes
but I still
want her
and
stay in
the cold Water
for one more hour
of porn
waiting for her
to come home

so
I can tell her
that I ran no
errands
and
did no cleaning
but
I want to fuck
and
I will be sad
and angry
when she says no
and
think that
her love
for me
is gone
and
say thank
god I masturbated
since you won't
fuck me
and
see this
is why I don't
run errands or clean
see
I need to use my
down time
to masturbate
in case you
don't fuck me

and
hey!
don't give me that
look
look
I even used that
cream on my balls
that makes the hair
go away
but
look
it made them red
and they burn
see
isn't that nice of me
look
what I did for you
see
look
see
look

she takes me
for granted

the water
isn't that cold
yet anyway

getting close

my therapist told me
he only thinks about
killing himself
once
every
two
years

he said
it is just a fleeting thought
that he acknowledges
and
then he
goes about his day
like it never entered his mind

I am getting close

suicide enters my mind
very little
compared to before
but
it still shows itself
when someone I love
gets upset
gets disappointed
gets depressed
or
when I feel trapped
and
my freedom is limited

instead of
removing
the situation
I think about
removing
myself

the thought
enters quickly

and
stays
until
the situation
fixes itself
or
the loved person
is happy

it makes me scared
to think
of what would happen
if the situation
or
if the person's
unhappiness
stayed unresolved

I am realizing
how fragile I am
and
how dependent I am
on other people's
happiness

or maybe
I am just a coward
that wants to run
instead of fight

I do not look
at overcoming -
I only look at
giving up

it is ironic
that the feelings
of empathy
and love
that make me
suicidal
are the same ones
that make me

unable to
pull the trigger

if I die
by my own hand
I am sure everyone will say
that I either
felt too much
or
that I was a coward

I think
it would be a mixture
of the two

I want
to be like my therapist
and
think about suicide
once
every
two
years

I tell myself this
whenever I get
depressed
but

I am not sure
if that is what
I really want

it feels hypocritical
to cause so much pain
on the ones
whose unhappiness
cause me pain

it doesn't make sense

but
neither does depression

to live is to die

let's see which
I do first

couch (the worst last name)

we bought
a new couch
and
in an attempt
to feel more
successful
than we are
    we
    bought
a modern couch
a $1,000   couch

and it is
very uncomfortable
-
especially to lay on
or
try to read on

the ends
are too high
        up
and too wide
so
your neck
is at an 87 degree
angle
and
hurts after 22 seconds

it is okay,
though
because I am often
        lazy
and would nap
on the couch
if I could
but
because I am often
        lazy
I do not walk up

a flight of stairs
to get to my bed

too much work
so
I stay on the couch
and fight
my lazy sleepiness
in order
to keep
reading
uncomfortably
drawing
uncomfortably
staring
uncomfortably
on the couch
that keeps me awake

but
I like to be awake

sleeping
gives me too much
        hope

Fortune cookie

snow day
and
the wife wants soup
for breakfast

I obliged
and while making said soup
I found leftover fortune cookies
from last nights chinese food

I figured a
        nice
        easy
snow day
was as good a time as any
for a look into my future,
or
some off-hand words of wisdom

I reached for the first cookie
opened it
and the fortune read
"Love is the affinity
which links and draws together
the elements of the world."

I felt nothing for that line -
all I felt love-wise
the last few months
was blue balls

I turned over the piece of paper
and
on the back
it said
"How about another Fortune?
SecondFortune.com"

Fortune
was capitalized -
fucking propaganda

I did want another Fortune,
however, but
looking one up online felt,
ironically,
too random,
and
like cheating

I spotted another cookie
on the counter

I grabbed it
tore it open
and
put
the worlds' worst tasting
communion wafer
in my mouth
(you have to eat it
or else the words mean nothing,
like guessing which finger
an eyelash is on correctly)

this second Fortune read,
"Where there is an open mind,
there will always be a frontier."

frontier? okay,
this was more my speed,
with the open mind and all,
but frontier?
what kind of frontier?

a dictionary search
brings up
"a line or border separating
two countries"

so where there is an open mind,
you'll be different than most?

hell,

it could even mean different from
a little,
that's all a frontier is -
a border between you and
a single entity,
technically

so I'm different than
SOMEONE

yeah,
no shit

jesus christ,
I should write these

worse than fucking
Hallmark

Bourdain

eat
drink
smoke
travel
talk
and walk

like Bourdain

just don't love
like him

chupacabra

what if the lengends are true
      the myths
      the folklore

what if our bodies are immortal
and there is no natural death

car accidents, suicide, overdose
murder,
cancer is a mutation
like a tumor

and heart attacks
are not from old age
or diet
but from seeing
outside of this dimension

we wake in the night
to see the face of
vampires
ghosts
ghouls
undead
and the shock
paralyzes us
and makes everything stop
working

what if everything is real
and there is no such thing
as a work of fiction

heel turn

I get confused
and find myself
jumping
    like a rabbit
back
  and
forth
between Being
humble
confident
cocky
self-doubting

what is the difference
between
confident
and
cocky

if I know my worth
would that not make me
cocky

if I am humble
does that not mean
I doubt my worth

I go to extremes
never settling on one

I do not know
which is correct
and which is
which

heels are confident/cocky

baby faces doubt

both are annoying

I can't pick
the wrong one
if I don't talk

then you'll never know
what I think
about myself

we can assume
together

closer.

I traded in
land surveying
for
residential counselor I
at a teenage
female group
        home

closer.

but that means
everything is done

the band is done
my social life is done
writing is done
sex is done

I live here now

closer.

longer than
nine to five
and different numbers
too

but that means
that I'm

closer.

to my
professional goal

since it is done

and the band
will get famous
without me
and my friends

will find other friends
and poetry will
remain unreadable
and my friends
will find other friends

and the girls
will get no

closer.

number five

maybe I've hit my low point -
fucking an addict
that I met
at an HIV testing clinic

she was number five
and I was number seven

I was numb
while
pumping into her

I guess I did it for spite
but it was pointless
since you don't know I'm here

I realized this
while the skeleton was on top -
your favorite position

I didn't cum

I hope they
forgive me

there's no beauty in sanity

you
drive me
crazy

good thing
there's
no beauty
in sanity

ayatollah

sitting at a beer garden
on a beautiful
fall day
wind blowing
a book on the table

and everyone around me
keeps mentioning
my
tattoos
or
my
book

but

my body is
covered
and
my book
is face down

yet everyone
talks about
the beatles
professional wrestling
dexter
hitchcock
cobain
bourdain

and they talk
while looking at me
but
I am hidden

I think
while
nursing my beer

maybe they all know

me
maybe twilight zone
maybe sims
maybe black mirror

or

maybe
I relate to everyone

maybe
I have something
for everyone

maybe
my
name
will be the next

out of their mouths

BMW

the lawn is manicured
the dishes are done
the mail has arrived

my neighbor
on the left
gets in his BMW
while the birds sing

and the mansion
on my right
has a real estate agent
and an aggressive,
entitled woman
with a bitch face
standing outside

the bitch is yelling
about how she can
afford more
and how she deserves
more
and she is
more more more
and
the real estate agent
tries to calm her
focusing on her
commission

and
in hopes
of lowering the value
of my community
and myself
I burp loudly
fart
scratch my balls
wave with the same hand
and
go back inside

there's only room for one
unworthy rich person
in this community

did I get too fat?

why don't you go
read...
or write
or paint
or anything else
that you brag about
and
leave
me
alone

I can't tell
if she really wants
me to leave her alone
so I touch
her arm
and kiss her
head

go away!

so I go away
and try to read
but
after a while
I get bored
and curious
more curious
so I walk back to
her

oh my god
I'm going outside
don't follow me

don't you love me

why are you so
annoying

I only said

good morning

at the airport

"I'm a poet."
I tell the bartender,
    the traveler,
        the lady sitting next to me
at the airport.

They say,
"Impressive! Inspiring!
Are you doing readings?
Are you published?"

"Yes.

Bukowski,
Eliot,
Whitman,
Cohen,
Dylan,
Cummings,
Ginsberg,
Masso.

I'm a poet."

I say my line,
look down at my drink,
take a sip,
sigh,
and wait for my stomach
to hurt,

because it always hurts
when I lie.

checkmate

this world is too overwhelming. cancel culture. digging up pasts, not given freedom to make mistakes or grow. inflation. money ruling happiness. goals are no longer attainable. passions come and go. human nature is put behind society's structure. to see the world you get two weeks a year to do so. but you must earn those two weeks after you work ten hours a day at a job that means nothing to you for at least a year. so much of life is done for others or distraction. we work to afford distractions from our work. we live to avoid dying. some die to avoid living. avoidance is what keeps the economy going. small talk to get through the day so we don't sit in our own heads. we spend twenty hours a day sleeping or working only to see our family for four hours, two of which are for chores or cooking. we can't see a therapist who works nine to five because we work nine to five. we can't go to a gym after work or else we wouldn't see our family at all. or, to create more time, we never sleep and die in single car crashes. we have an urge to post what we do, where we go, what we write so others can see it. that's the new normal. that's the new instinct. gone is any thought of doing something for yourself. gone is knowing how to be alone. we can text and talk at any time. We can scroll, watch videos, see what everyone is doing. we can see all the positive and all the negative without filters - and with filters. there's too many contradictions. we've evolved too quickly. three years away from ready player one. five years away from every black mirror episode. i don't want to be here for that. so i go into the woods. but i won't. i'm conditioned to care that people will view me as a freak. i'm a domestic dog, unequipped for survival in the wild. i'm anxious, depressed, and always scared. our brains are not the same as they were in our past. we no longer want children. we no longer want to hunt. we no longer want to survive. i no longer want to survive. it's a losing game we are playing. we put ourselves in checkmate.

hangover days

we work
for the hangover
days

the days after
we spend our paycheck
on beer
and
food and gas

and explore
and drink
and fuck

and wake up
in sweat
and semen
and drool

we work
for the hangover
days

the days
wasted
staying in bed
naked
and in pain

and shitting
and vomiting
and showering

and going back
to bed
to watch porn
and
cursing ourselves

and thinking
about the work

week
ahead

we work
for the hangover
days

the days
feeling like
we made it
and
wondering
why we haven't

the days
of weight gain
and fat loss

and we wait
until the afternoon
when we feel
good
enough to
do it again

we work
for the hangover
days

the days
of a sunday
and monday
to be spent
like kings

the days
run wild
and we give up
our dreams
for two hangover days

the hangover days
the hangover days

the shitting
the yelling
the fucking
the sleeping
the spending
the working

we work
for the hangover
days

until
we learn to
work
on
the hangover days

mean girls

what's the limit
    with sex

I don't know,
   I told them

maybe porn
maybe rape

maybe we are animals
so there is none

maybe if you can't
focus on work
or production

maybe thinking
is cheating

can you sleep at night
or are you
burning yourself
with yesterday's
iron prod

if the little things
     in life
  get me off,
then my testosterone
is too low,
    I'm a dork.
if I want to fuck
all the time,
I am a monster/I am
- - - - - - - - - -

exit stage left.
standing ovation.
return stage right.
take a bow.

I walk into the night
to find myself a
whore.

idols

your mind will change
like the ringing
in your pocket

your mind will see reason
and you will
regret
the ink
in your skin
and the posters
and the dreams

if you want
to keep your idols
do not read them
do not watch them
and most importantly
do not become famous
like them

you will see the drugs
not as a needed pain
or muse in place
of women

but
as weakness
or poor percentage
of creativity

the body
not made from
money
but sleep deprivation
and
no one at home
to cook for them

they change too

from

democrat to republican
from
young to old
from
jailbirds to pastors
from
alive to dead

and when that happens
you change

no one is god
no one is emotionless
no one is

be influenced
by the idea
not the person

when
    the idols
fall away
you
are only
left
with you

rebound

I think ultimate
maturity
and the key
to a happy life
is

how you handle
the end
of
your last
relationship

instead of
thinking about
who is
fucking her
now,

you think
about who is
enduring
her
talking,
snoring,
money-spending,
and other problems

remember the bad
and fuck
somebody else's
mistake

the bandaid

too many poems about
death
too many poems about
working
not enough poems about
sex

my wife has
the best tits
the tightest pussy
and
the greatest mouth

but she doesn't like
my sex poems -
well
not publicly -

so it's back to
work
and
death

the two things
that come after
the fucking

the two things
that come after
each other

sex
is the
bandaid

work
is the
wound

death
is the

cure

and nobody
wants to be
cured

triple j

I am dressed in all black
slick and groomed
with whitened teeth
being driven two hours away
to be in a music video
with all strangers
and
on the drive
we are listening to foreign
radio stations
and I want to travel
and I am confident
that I will
and I feel famous
and energized
and free
and like I'm
supposed to be here
and tomorrow
I'm supposed to not
be

the dog deserves better

it has been
nine days without
beer

so that wasn't
the problem/ only
the problem

I am still
angry
all the time
at the dog
at the cat
at the cold
at the process
at the working
at the sleeping
at the mirror
at the traffic
at the money
at the sex
at the food
at the wind
at the phone
at the body
at the mind

I am still
taking shortcuts
I am still
lazy

I am still
avoiding the snow
and the sun

I am still
avoiding the better
and the worse

I am still

not reading
barely writing

I am still
who
is
by fire

I am still
looking
for the answer

the quick fix

begging it is
not you

anything but
    you

anything but
    us

lie, lie, lie

i lied to you
about getting rid
of my gun

i still have it
i still don't plan
on using it

but it's there
and it cannot be
thrown away

or discarded
like your scars
it still gets shown
to me

even when everything
is perfect

even when the sun
is out
it can still
rain

without reason
without cause

and i wish it
would only rain
on me

and not you
as well

but the rain
makes us
love the clear days
even more

and hopefully

over time
we
and
i
can learn how to
live
without being hindered
by the weather

and dance in it
and remember
that
it can't rain all the time

blue-balls

back and forth
back and forth
up and down
up
   and
       down

moan

in   out
she
   grabs the cushion
and grits
   her teeth

i grab
   her ass
pull
it in
then   up
then in
then   up

i grab her
flip her
lay down
she
gets on   top

back and forth
back and forth

she grabs my
chest
and puts her nails
in
and
   down

and screams
and falls on   top

she breathes
heavily

and slowly gets up
and
my cock falls
out of her

and she looks at
me
while she grabs her
shirt and
her
pants

and she walks
    away

she blue-balled
me

and i
lay there
staring
at nothing

angry?
then

i smile
i feel

proud of her

Omega

I'm tired of
losing to
laziness

and
I want to be
Omega
and reach
the peak
of myself

and I want to
breathe
fuller and fresher

so I take
my books
to a coffee shop
and act like
an author
for a few hours

and
I put on
an Orson Welles
film
because
exercising your mind
is better than
your body

the body
comes next
for I
fall in love
too deeply
with content
     complacency
     cockiness

and my hunger

for greatness
returns
but this time
it is focused
and realistic
and grown up

and now I want to
work
full time
all the time
on my body
on my mind
on my art
on my work ethic
on my love
and
I want to transcend
like a balloon
and distance
myself from the dirt
and the earth
and the rest of the
helium bags
tied to chairs
and buildings
and gravestones

but I could
distance myself
from you
as well
and
I don't want to
so I stay lazy
afraid
that you will not
climb
with me
and once I get too far
you will
lose sight of me

like a stone
thrown into the ocean
or
a star behind
a cloud

the brighter I shine
the less you will look
the less you will see
until I shine so bright
your eyes can take no more

and I burn out
and you fade away

Nathaniel

I'm falling back into that place
           no job
           no money
           no passion

sex has
stopped working
and
I'm looking for
vices again

tax return for cigarettes
and
school debt without a
degree

too many hobbies
and
no career

walking alone
and
engaged to you
      to masses

yesterday's don't help
the present
but
history repeats itself

once an addict
always an addict

I wonder if you
thought of that
or if you signed up
for it

nine get rich quick
schemes

nine credit cards
maxed

nine lives
and
nine to go

wake up,
Nathaniel

It's time to put your
suit on
and
face another funeral

hide

it always goes back
    to hiding

in the shower
in your car
in the bathroom
at work

hiding the sins
and the laughter
and
the desires
and fantasies

and
what you need
to be happy
stays a secret
too

I need
this
this moment
hiding
behind a door
        any door
and
just writing
my heart
my truth
my taboo

I'm not lazy
I'm just
afraid
of the clock
and
afraid of
failure

so I hide

from those
fears

and write you
a new
suicide note
everytime
I do

models

"because i know
what is going to happen!

i'm going to work
until eight o'clock
and come home
and the dogs
will follow me around
and you will have
already eaten
and you will scroll
through your phone
      alone
for four hours
opposite me
on the couch
and i will
reluctantly play video
games and watch
a documentary
that I would rather
watch with you
just so i can be
next to you
and the cat
will jump up
and block the
television anyway
and the dogs
will make me get up
four times
to let them out
so i will never
relax anyway
and then at midnight
we will go to bed
and not fuck
since we haven't talked
or touched all day
and i will
lie in bed awake

dreading the same
thing tomorrow
and the day after

so yes
i want to go to
the bar after work
because at least
that is new every day
and exciting
and unpredictable
and at least i will
talk to people
and feel like
something happened
in my fucking life."

she stared at me,
blank.

"i'll sleep on the
couch."

i grabbed a pillow
and blanket
and watched a
documentary
about a mountain
i will never climb

Bag of Scum

I am
a
scum bag.

a cliche, positive poem

there is good nights
to be had

good conversations
that keep us alive

if you do not
force them

the bad times
end

the good times
come back

if you do not
force them

they will love
you

if you do not
force them

fantasies become
realities

and all those
cliches

lesson learned
and implemented

hopefully
like the poem

don't try
try not to

making his way to the ring...

you would think
creating a character
would be easy for
someone like me

and it was
when I was
younger
wilder
dumber
weaker
     and
shy-er

I had plenty
of characters
and ideas
and names
and hats

but
now that I am
becoming
the person
that
I want to be
more
and
more
closer
and
closer

and
now that I am
drinking water
instead of beer
and
muscular
instead of fat
and

working
instead of lazy

I am losing
the need
for a new name
for a new attitude
for a new mask

I am
me

and I like me

for the most part

happy with that

it's very hard
     for me
to sit still,
especially while
traveling

I love hotel rooms
and cabins
and rooms
that are not mine

but I want
the foreign
to continue

I want to
be at new places
constantly

new restaurants
new breweries
new shops
new cafes
new grocery stores

and
my wife
is the opposite

she wants a new cabin
with her old dogs
and she is happy with that

so we compromised
and take turns having
vacations

mine in constant motion -
hers in constant stillness

and she moves with me

without hesitation
or complaint

and I always fail
to return the favor

I always get greedy
and antsy
and selfish
and complain
that we could be doing
more
and experiencing
more
and I make her
vacations
    a little like hell
and she makes mine
perfect

I crave what I am not
in her
and in travel

which do I hold
more dear

sacrifices.

he sat on my couch
and we drank wine -
me more than
him -
as he talked
and talked
and talked
about all the girls

"yeah I got cold feet
so what?
I've done so many
broads now.
I never got to do that
before, ya know?"

"yeah,
so do you miss her?"

"I mean, I don't
want to think
of her
suckin' some other guy
off and stuff,
ya know,
I mean, I know what
she's capable of."

"she was good for you."
I drank another glass
without offering him any

"no, no, look
I had all types last week.
they all feel so different.
it's fun, it's fun
and stereotypes
hold up for all them!
like..."

"I get it.

you made a mistake,
though."

"no, didn't you
think about what
you'd be missing?
didn't you watch
porn and crave
the chase, the freedom?"

"yes, but she's good
for me
and she was good
for you."

"she held me back.
how could I travel
or be an artist?"

"I'm an artist."

"but travel.
I don't want to be
told what to do
or be yelled at
for stupid things!"

"sacrifices.
they are always right.
when I get yelled at
I deserve it.
I'm off drugs
and I'm not dead.
she was good for you."

"freedom is good for me.
pussy is good for me.
anymore wine?"

"no, I'm about to
finish it."

"give me a tad."

"no.
so what comes next?
where are you traveling to?"

"I don't know,
she made the money."

"right."

"I don't know how
you married."

"I'm a sell-out."

"wanna go to the bar?"

"no."

he left
and I took out
another bottle of wine

cheers to those
brave enough
to not marry
and
foolish enough
to not care

next

my friends
keep getting divorced
and
I keep consoling
while
my fear grows
worse and worse

and
statistics say
that I am
next

and
statistics say
that we are
next

and
statistics say
that you are
next

and while
freedom sounds
like a great thing
to have,

I realize
that love is
the only religion
I need to believe
in

the blowjob mystery

he said
that he was given
oral sex
by a family member
when he was seven

and now he has
a deep love
for blowjobs

"don't get me wrong
I love pussy,
but nothing makes
me feel better
than a BJ.
I can be a little
rough, though,
ya know, so maybe
that's why she doesn't
do it too often."

yes, I thought,
everybody loves
a one-way road

he swears
that the
family member
was real,
but the rest of
his family says
no

they told him,
"he never ever ever
came over our house
let alone babysat
you."

now I want to find
out the truth

not for him,
but for me,
and for all gentlemen
everywhere

were we all molested
or are blowjobs
just that
good

the piano movers

"those who can't do teach"
he says
and passes me
the bottle of wine

"sure, but he can't teach either.
tell your wife to get more wine"

he asks her, she goes
I watch her go
I watch for too long

"masso!"
he screams
"ya know, for someone
who thinks he's god
your name doesn't
sound iconic"

"I don't know
what my name is"
I stand and look
for the bathroom.
I fall on the way there
and hit my elbow
on a bookshelf

"fuck"
I say

"masso, after you
piss shit or die
in my bathroom
come tell me why
you hate me
and the world"

I died in his bathroom
then came out
and fell on the recliner,
grabbed the bottle

and said
"piano movers make
$50/hr"

"do you want to move pianos?"

"no"

"then why do you care"

"I'm a god with a shit name"

"change it"

"no"

"you are no god"

"I am, I just don't get paid
like it"

we sat in silence
until his wife
came back with more wine
and she gave me a bottle
and I drank half
and said
"your wife likes Leonard Cohen"

he said that I was correct

"I'm going to drink
too much to drive"

"stay here"
he said
"and keep talking"

"I want to leave
my job again"

"but it pays well"

"my boss can't teach or do"

"not many can"

"Hm"

"Hm"

I walk upstairs
and lay on his bed -
the bed they fuck in.
tonight they will fuck
on the couch

and I will not
fuck anyone
besides myself
again and again
again and again
again and

ode to fucking

when you see a wheelchair
or some poor fucked-up fucker
the first thing to come to mind is
"will they ever fuck?"

probably not -
but you can

so don't waste that luxury

sober

the scene on this beach
is so calming
with my feet
unseen
under the sand
and
I'm shirtless
even with my beer belly
and
my mouth
is wide open
spilling secrets
and
genuinely
laughing

I feel
absolutely
no anxiety

what a feeling

I wonder
if I'll ever feel this
without alcohol

I didn't eat lunch yet

I have blue jeans on
like a country song
like Brett Favre

and I'm outside
smoking
and listening
to the birds

wondering why I
put myself
through these
ten hour days

and I look at
grass
trees
swaying

and I close
my eyes
to meditate

and I think
of my patience
and my house
and how money
works

and I see it
now
the meaning
of life

acceptance
I think

and I dig deeper
trying to change
my view forever

trying to make
sure
acceptance
is the key

and…

break is over.

deerskin

it's hard to feel more at home
writing
on a leather couch
next to a deerskin lamp
with trees printed on it
a fireplace next to the lamp
warming your legs
in a cabin

you smell like smoke
from the fire
you just made
outside

outside
where the lake is your front yard
and where
the mountains
held your feet
just one hour
ago

you close your eyes
open them

you are back in the cabin
with a blank canvas
in your hands

and you remember
who you are
when you are not
in the city
when you are not
at a 9-5
when you are not
stuck

yes
it's hard to feel more at home

when you are
finally
with yourself
again

coco

tomorrow
i will start tomorrow
and the day after that
and by day four
i will be
proud of myself
and worthy
of love

i will stop
drinking
and chasing
and lying
and sloth-ing

i will lose weight
and overcome
my addictions
all of them
immediately
cold turkey
whatever that means

and i will
be healthy
mentally
and
physically

and excuses
will end
and i will
look
and
act
and
speak
and
work
and
fuck

like a god

i promise
you

i will start
tomorrow

you sounded good

you beg me to send a postcard.
and I do not.
I miss the letters, but I don't miss
the lies behind them. you never did
a damn thing you wrote about. it sounded
good, though, oh, it sounded damn good.
I wanted them to publish you so bad
and it finally happened and I cared a lot,
but not how you would have thought.
I was filled with rage,
until I realized who the publisher was. and
when I read it and saw the amount you
stole from me, I laughed, and drank four beers
very quickly. I was never bothered by a poets'
success or work, mostly because I never
thought it was any good. but yours is hard
to swallow. it is good, and it is upsetting,
and I thought you were good.
but in your good book by the good publisher
you had a forty page section dedicated
to all the poets and artists you adored. and I
was not in it. and for some reason it hurt
and opened wounds while closing them.
our smoke came together from three
thousand miles away, as did our dreams.
oh, you had me. by the balls and the wallet.
I paid for you to go places I haven't been yet.
and you went without me. but you made me
feel good, like I had it all. and I didn't even have
you. a sugar daddy without a job.
I'm sure our books will sit on the shelves
next to each other's. can you imagine? one a
drunk, one a whore. both actors. I didn't get
to fuck you, but that's okay, because I realized
that I didn't want to for any wholesome reason.
it would have been for what you represented, and
then it would have been for punishment. I wonder
who is taking more punishment now. probably
my wife. my poor wife. innocent in our lives. clawing
herself to be heard over your ghost and my
dream catcher. and she works to pay my bills

while I sit at a bar rereading the poems you wrote
about me, especially the ones that say you still
love me, and she wears our wedding ring while
I text you, three thousand miles away, five years
away. and you don't answer. at least not until
she is off work and sees your name light up
on my phone. yes, the innocent suffer the most.
while we both wish it was different,
but are grateful for how it is.

start writing

two options come up
when I open my computer

choose template
start writing

I always hit
start writing

just start writing

and see where it takes you

and today
it took me
to this shit poem

steel-toe

our bodies are capable
of so much -
just look at Ozzy
or the Arnold

yet
when I put on
those work boots -
black
tired
caked
without mercy
-
my body fights back
by developing
a hangover
or
aching at the age
of twenty-two

I suddenly feel tired
and suicidal
like a snake
wrapped around
a clock
and
what does it matter
when my money
goes to wine
and cigarettes
and sex
and music
and anything
to cope with
those boots

so marry a doctor
because even your
dream job
turns into a nightmare
sometimes

and none of us
are paid enough
to deal with it

afraid

to overcome reality
you need art
       drugs
   and love

and the ratio
can vary

but when
you work
a job
you hate
and
your house leaks
and there is mold
and your car no longer
starts
and your insurance
is more than
your paycheck
and
you do too much
of the second
fix
and you need more
fix
but nothing can be
fixed
not even your love

is art enough

what
and who
is right

the homeless
or
suicide
or
money

but money can't buy love
or art
or even some drugs

and the love
of another
or
of self

doesn't pay enough
to buy anything

nothing pays enough
to buy anything

so the homeless
or
the dead
have the answers

and everyone is afraid
of both

a fly in the mansion

my muscle mass
is gone
I am weak
and frail
but fatter
than I have ever
been
and
I have not
showered
in four days
maybe five
and
this happened
last week
and
last week
and
I am lazy
-er than ever
but
I finally have
a career
in a field
of passion
and
I'm young
for the field
and
it's what I
dreamed of
but
my dreams change
too quickly
too often
so
nothing is
ever good enough
like a new car
like a new fuck
the next day

will be better
but
the grass
is never greener
when you
hate yourself
but have an ego
or
when you
think a fly
in your mansion
means that
the mansion
is crap
and
you are crap
and
that one extra
dollar
or
that one extra
trip overseas
or
that one extra
blowjob
will be why
life is okay
life is worth it
life is a gift
a gift
like socks
or underwear
when you're six
years old
and
you don't
forget
or
forgive
those gifts
or
those laughs
or

that time
you were mean
to your mother
as a toddler
no forgiveness
no forgetting
no healing
no solace
in maturing
because
you are never
mature enough
you are never
rich enough
you are never
wanted enough
you are never
tough enough
and
you are never
good enough
to let
anything be
good enough

2020

my wife and I
decided to buy a house
but the government
and mortgage people
made it take
three months
then four
then five

then the virus
adds on
month six
then my job is lost
and
then her job is lost

then we need
to pay the
down payment
with no jobs
so we give all we have
but the house
is still not ours
until she works again

now we are down
to one car
and no house

and she uses the car
to finally go back
to work

and on the day
before
we are to close
we get into
a car accident

now we need
to pay for two cars

to pay the mortgage
to pay the utilities
to pay for food
to pay for gas
to pay for houseware
to pay the government

and the government
won't let us work
or help
or
delay the money
going into
their pockets
while we sell
our pockets
for food

with
no car
no house
no hope

the car accident
broke
her ring
and
broke
my will

but since she is working
we finally get the house
and two weeks
after we move in
someone smashes her
car window

now we need
to pay for two cars
to pay for one window
to pay the mortgage
to pay the utilities
to pay for food

to pay for gas
to pay for houseware
to pay the government

and then the next day
her muffler falls off

now we need
to pay for two cars
to pay for one window
to pay for one muffler
to pay the mortgage
to pay the utilities
to pay for food
to pay for gas
to pay for houseware
to pay the government

and to make money
you need to spend
              money

judgement-free

I do not judge the criminals
the crooks
the thieves
the petty crime
and the murderers
the traffic ticket
and the arson

I do not judge the disabled
the slow
the mundane
the accidents
and the addicts
the suicides
and the attempts

I do not judge the secrets
the characters
the lust
the adultery
and the gambling
the child porn
and the incest

I do not judge
for
I have been some of these
and will end up being more

striped shirts and mini skirts

she took the stage
and sounded like the
New York punk scene
of the 70's

Debbie Harry clothing
The Dead Boys attitude
Patti Smith poetry
CBGB

I liked that
I liked that she was raised,
or raised herself,
on that music

you don't just stumble
upon that music

you have to search for it
      be broken for it

you have to
    have
empathy for the innocent
empathy for the addicts
empathy for the bankrupt
empathy for the normal

she took the stage
and sounded like the
New York punk scene
of the 70's

and not a single
soul
watched her

the reason(?)

I saw you
under Seattle's lights
singing for the birds,
but your song soon became
that of a siren's

I kept hearing your voice
whisper in my ear,
"why haven't you fallen in love
with me
yet?
pick something
you can tolerate
about me
and focus only on that"

I puzzled over these words
as I sat on dead animals

why am I forcing myself
to love you?

do I like having someone to chase
since that keeps me sad?
do I just want someone
to sleep with?
do I want to be under
Seattle's lights with you?

no,
if those reasons were correct
they'd be confident
enough to end
with periods,
not question marks

I am forcing myself
to love you
because someone
just stopped
loving me

and I need to believe that
everything happens
for a reason

capitol hill

bills
bills
the death of freedom

the reason we work
the reason for suicide
the reason they kill

forty hours a week
taken from our lives
because of ego
      and greed
and we become
hard and
miserable
from doing something
torturous - something
we don't want to do

forty hours a week

HALF OF OUR LIVES

christ.
don't blame the suicides

but I look
to my right
and she is laying
on her stomach
naked
and I am
naked
and she
is filling out a bill
to take to the post office
later
after one more round
of love-making
and it is worth it

they can have half of me

Takotsubo

it's a powerful thing
that out of billions
of people
there is one
that defies your hatred
for the rest

they are a fairy
in a war zone

the sweat
shit
piss
puke
imperfections of skin
breath of death

none of it matters
or exists
or repulses you
like it does when you look
at any other human being

you can't understand
why anyone would pick
someone who isn't her

you stop looking at porn
because only she
turns you on
-
at least for
a while

you think about
the sweat
shit
piss
puke
of everyone else

you view death
as more welcome
than a life without her -
as if you weren't alive
before you met her

you are sure
that not one person
out of billions
would fill her role

your memories
before her
are blurry
and feel as if
someone else lived them
her lips
feel like heroin
and her arms
are more comforting
than a blanket
and her body
is more appetizing
than any model
or god

and it's a
dangerous game
but it is worth playing

so you play
and you play
and you can't stop
you don't want to stop

the sex
the showers
the dinners
the laughter
the jealousy
the money
the lack thereof
the yelling

the singing
the dancing

and you play
until one of you
dies
and then
the other dies
months later
from a broken heart

and you pray
that love
is more than
just
  chemicals.

thursday in december

I worked
as a land surveyor
and it was a
thursday in
december
and like most days
we were sent out in pairs
and I was with a real
anxious type,
clean shaven,
not yet thirty,
and he would tell
me about his life -
every detail -
and I listened
and nodded
and he was mostly happy

but this was a
thursday in
december
and I pulled the van
to the side of the road
and we got out to measure
a few trees
and he was telling me
how his girl was mad at him
and wouldn't cuddle
and wouldn't talk to him
and he didn't know why
she was being so petty
and I listened
and nodded
and he was real hurt

he lived for his girl
and he knew she loved him
but he needed
to be shown it
(perhaps too often)
and I asked him to move

the van
the next block down
and when he got
into the drivers seat
a car came speeding
down the hill
and lost control
and devastated the
drivers side of
the van

and on the next
thursday in
december
we laid him to rest
and I saw his girl
sobbing and shaking
and she started telling me
that she didn't get to say
goodbye
and that she hoped
he knew
how much
she loved him
and that she couldn't live
with herself, oh
how could she be
so petty
so childish
and she cried
and she cried
and I listened
and nodded

too little

it fascinates me
that I don't know
how
or
what
to write
when I feel
suicidal

like there is
nothing to say

or perhaps
there is

too much

the death of Dick Clark

three hours before
the ball drops
and a new year begins
and my phone keeps
ringing
and people keep
telling me to come
to their parties
with booze
and babes
and big cigars
and I tell them no
and they ask
over and over again
why
and I look at my wife
sitting on the couch
with her dogs
in her nightwear
bra-less and bare feet
and she does not like
parties
and I tell the phone ringers
no
because I said no
and I hang up
and wait for the next
phone call

but I cannot blame them
for expecting my presence

last New Year's Eve
I was snorting blow
with whores

this New Year's Eve
I am happy

inside a barn-like house

case closed
case reopened
like the window
that let in
mosquitos
mosquitos
buzzing around my ear
around my coffin
loved in life, buried alone
throw her on top
like a cherry
like a raindrop
on the bird's feathers
like the raccoon
in the days old food
look at the yellow
kaleidoscope to
red to blue to
nothing as
Shakespeare sleeps
Camus sleeps
Fitzgerald sleeps
and she's read none of them

putty pulled from the wall
stop signs illuminated by
headlights
of cars driving
to Atlantis
to Mars
to distances as far
as stoves
and dinosaurs

but she knows not
of history
and why should she
the past a couch
and a stairwell

and

monks drink beer
and the sky stays blue

one more

after not paying rent
for three months
and my wife
cutting off my beer fund
I decided it may
be time
to find a job

so I scheduled
a few interviews
and after missing
the first two
I showed up to the third
with messy hair and
unshaven beard

the boss was younger
than me and had
a GQ jawline
along with a shark's smirk
and barbershop eyes
and he asked for my resume
and I handed it to him
and he looked it over
and said, "you worked
a lot with animals and
retail. maybe you
should stick to that
because you have no
experience in any
other industry."

and I said, "I would
have experience if anyone
gave me a shot. and I can
no longer work with animals
because the smell is horrible
when you are hungover
and retail is for the untalented."

he asked what skills

I had gained from my
past jobs
and
the answer was none
because I glided by
and
he smirked
that punchable smirk
and I clenched my fist
and he said
that I should stay
with the animals
and the retail
and the talentless
and the teenagers
and I stood up
and said thank you

and Trump's unemployment
rate rose one more number

worthless

I
am a wreck

I
am a disgrace
   a disgusting
 slob

who should probably
be categorized
as a murderer
or thief
of some kind

a man
who goes home
after a half-assed
work day
and watches porn
until my hands
are sticky

a man
who steals
to pay off credit card debts
and stops at bars
too many days
a week

a man
who will be
selfish
and end up
killing himself
for ego
or lust
or laziness
regardless of
the love
or perfection
my life grants me

run away,
far away,
before the bomb
ticks for the last time

there is no power here

there is no future

there is cum
    and betrayal
      and disappointment
    and death

and like my poetry
I am worthless

pimples

I arrived home
to a depressed
and angry
    wife

she needed to move
she needed a new job
she needed money

I tried to talk
to her
but the stress was too much

I ate dinner silently
while she laid in bed

when I joined her
I thought that
I'd let her
pop some pimples on my back
(she had an obsession
  with those damn things)

she sat up
and really squeezed
the first one

then the next
 and the next

she squeezed
with every ounce of strength
that she had

she dug her nails
into my back

I could almost hear
the screaming
she was keeping inside

"That's fine, baby,"
I said,
"take it out on me."

she squeezed harder
            and harder

and I finally turned around
and grabbed her face
and kissed her
and she kissed back
and my tongue found her throat
and she returned the favor
and we made love
and we were animals
and we were primal
and we were passionate
and sweat covered the sheets
and blood covered the sheets
and we laid in it
and held hands
and held each other
and felt it

and tomorrow she needed money

wine and cheese

intermission
at an internally-renowned
male vocal choir
show

and I am outside with the
smokers
trying to fit in
with my nicest
Goodwill clothes
and they speak of getting
wine and cheese
after the concert
and it makes me sick
although wine and cheese
sound good

we go back inside
for the second act
and they finger-snap
instead of applaud
and it makes me sick
although I am jealous
that I cannot snap
and after the performance
they speak of how amazing
it was
while they wipe their eyes
and drool from their mouths

and everyone
is an actor

green vests

those green vests
neon and indecent

at the substations
at the intersections
at the manholes
and telephone wires
those green vests

are evil
and drunk
and empty
and they die
alone
and without travel

and
I
am now one
of them
and I am conflicted
if I want to be

I am evil
and drunk
but I care too much
to be alone
and empty
and I must travel

I am the youngest
and I am
stupid
and I hear the jokes
and endure the shouts
expecting me to
be better
like it's easy
and it is
if you are
alone

and
etc.

but I am not

I read in the work
truck
while they talk
about sports
and bills
and they
joke and shout
about my books
and poetry
and maybe I am
too feminine
to wear a green vest
and that is okay
with me

I will listen
and endure
until I am fired
or
famous

I need the paycheck
to travel
and to get
drunk

that simple

wake up
take a piss
go to the cupboard
and find
that there is
no coffee
take out a cigarette
and walk outside
and the landlord is there
screaming and flailing
and yelling
and spitting
walk past him
to the car
and it won't start
and the wife won't answer
your phone call
because she hates
your face
and the bar is
walking distance
and you walk
and you arrive
and you drink
and you spend
the last fifty dollars
on booze
instead of a battery

and everyone's advice is
Get. A. Job.

Jameson

in a basement
full of beer cans
and ashtrays
we sat discussing
art and music
and who should be famous
and who should not

and a friend of a friend
of a friend of a friend
took a seat
and grabbed my Jameson
and took a swig
and I should have hit him
but I did not

and he listened to us
talk
and complimented my art
and poetry
and would say
"Yeah!"   "Definitely!"
"Oh, Totally!"
whenever we finished
a sentence

and I could tell he was drunk
but I gave him the benefit
of the
doubt
and then he started
flirting
horribly
with the girls
and I lit a cigarette
and he followed
and I mentioned Rimbaud
and he said he was familiar
and he copied my every move
clearly unaware
of how to spell

art

and I kept staring at him
and he kept flirting
and saying
"That is absolutely right!"
and
"Art comes from the heart,
man!"

and I poured him a shot
of Jameson
and he drank it
and smiled
and I got up
and grabbed him by the neck
and opened the front door
and threw him
into the dark winter
night

history

I understand why
Hunter S. Thompson
shot himself
whenever
I turn
on the TV
and see

Trump.

magnanimous

we decided to take a nap
and I was the first one
awake
and I noticed
a moon
and stars
a full bladder
and a headache
from lack of cheap food
and too much cheap alcohol

her head
was pinning down
my arm
so
I had to decide
between letting her sleep
or
potentially waking her up

I looked at her face
        her hair
            her chest

and
I let her sleep

since she has to
go to work

and I do not

just one

i wish
i could have
a beer

just one

and sit
at a brewery
at 1pm
in the sun
and laugh
and enjoy
the beer

just one

and then
      go home
and clean
      or cook
or live
      like normal
like
everyone else
i'm watching
do
   right now
at
  my brewery

w-r-r-i-i-g-t-h-e-t

I'm supposed to write, right?
write when I want to write
write when I don't want to write
write when I'm not alright
write when I am alright
write right now
right now I should write
write about right now
write about her being right
write about her not being right
write about me being right
write about no one being right
write about writing
right on
write on
write
right?
——>

two day withdrawal

day two at
a hotel that
is too fancy for me

and I drink and
walk and walk
and drink and
drink and walk
and finally get
into bed

and I want to
write and drink
and drink and
write and I want to
write about sex
and how much I miss
her
and I want to describe
for me for her
for everyone
for no one
how her skin
feels and tastes and smells
and how her breasts
feel and taste and look
and how her pussy
feels and tastes and sounds
and how good she is
with my cock
in her hand in her mouth
and how she admires
my body my cum my love
and how none of this
would matter
if it wasn't with her
and I sit alone counting
the minutes until
I see her feel her
taste her smell her

and I toast to
me her everyone no one
that she is mine
and not yours

un cafè

it's 70 degrees out
and I have an article due
and a book due
tonight
and I stare at my papers
then look outside
then think
of Bourdain

so I gather my papers
and I get in my car
and drive to a bar
with the windows open
and I spread my papers
across the bar
and order a beer
and a sweet tea
and I write
my article
my book
and some poems
about writing
with beer
music
and a breeze

and I take in the people
around me
and write a few more
poems

and for a day
I pretend I am a writer

Trophy

my back is my proudest trophy,
scratched with your red-polished
                                      nails

tomorrow

I am in a hotel room
in a state
I have never been in
and
I'm writing this poem
while she sleeps
next to me

I needed to travel
it has always done me -
and I hope
my poetry -
good

so we got this room
with the plan to
get drunk
and
get passionate

instead it is nine o'clock
and she is asleep
and I am not

I think I would have been
angry
when I was younger
or maybe just
when I was not with
her

but I'm learning
to love these moments
the most
and
to enjoy the quiet
and her breathing
and her warmth
and her face

we can get drunk

tomorrow

These Family Parties

it feels like
I haven't written
a poem
in years

so I grab my journal
at the 4th of July party

It's a family party -
or wannabe family
        party

my cousin's boyfriend
(who won't make it
to marriage)
is lighting fireworks
to my right
and the rest of them
are inside

eating meat

while I sit in a chair
by myself
smoking and
drinking

I'm starting to see
double
and am afraid to
stand

I'm growing tired
of drinking
like this
in order to attend
these family parties -
or wannabe family parties

but

I wish we had more of
these little get-togethers

I write when I feel alone

the days run wild...

I still don't know
how to handle sadness
or loneliness

like when my wife
is mad at me
or the world

I always push
     push
    push
   her

like the wind
against glass

and then she yells at me
or locks the door
and I am left
being angry at her
pouring myself a drink
and lighting a cigarette
cursing her

and then I calm down
once drunk
and realize I wasn't there
for her
because she wasn't
there for me

and that is not love
love is not one person
needing the other
to always be happy

but my happiness
is still in her hands
and
not in my own

and I daydream
about the bachelor
about Chinaski
and think of the dreams
that I sacrificed for her
poet wrestler artist

and then I calm down
once drunk
and realize that I was
none of these before her
and none of these without
her

and none of them now

because I was single once
and instead of art I drank
and instead of poetry I fucked
and instead of wrestling I injected

and had no money
and traveled less often

she is love
and on her end it is good

but I am an addict
and when her emotions
mask affection
for even one second,

I withdraw
into the bachelor

I stand in the shower
with the heat turned up
and I crouch down
and wait for the cops
to take me
and plan my suicide
and cry onto this page

with the knowledge
that I am more
happy now than
ever

Wisdom

we buried
an unknown talent
and a known
great man
and
I sat at the funeral
at a baptist church
being one of three
white men
and
I wasn't uncomfortable
being in a church
being alive
being sober

I was uncomfortable
knowing that he was
better than Brahms
better than Gretzky
better than Dali
and I realized
that if he was to die
without fame
or statues or documentaries
then what would I have to do
and how phenomenal
or lucky
would I have to be
to avoid
dying unknown
as well

being an artist
comes with difficulties
and unjustness relative
to politics -
if not worse than politics -
and so if I die
fortunate
and he did not,
it would not be

because I was
the better artist,

it would be because
my straw was
a little bit longer
than his

the poems that talk about struggle

I'm reading Bukowski
alone
while my girlfriend is at a concert

and I'm realizing that I love
the poems
that talk
about struggle,
    confrontation,
    the poor,
    the broken,
    the ghetto,

and I look outside
and see that it's getting dark.

I think about taking a walk
around town.

Maybe I'll share a cigarette
with a poor
    broken
    ghetto
    struggler,

maybe we'll have a confrontation,
maybe I'll get a poem.

I think about it,

don't do it,

and stay comfortable.

the new place

in a grey town
I long for
a conversation
in a cheap room
and I think that would cure
everything
a
good
conversation
in a cheap room
about cummings, plath,
pollock, the death of poetry,
and the birth
of cubic zirconium hearts

fill my room
with red laughter,
for
rent is higher than it should be
(how I long for Buk's
3 and a half dollar a week room)
and this town is no good
for Art,

give me what I lack
and the price of rent
may be easier to swallow
   like a watered down vodka
and the crows peck my books
and my wallet and my cats

and the crows peck my books
and my wallet and my cats

and I stare at her

I'm sitting on
the loveseat
reading poetry
that is better than mine
and she is across from me
doing a puzzle
under a tiny lamp
and her hair is pulled back
just right
and her face is lit
just right
and I look at her hands
at work
and her finger without a ring
and I stare at her
and I stare at her
and I think about
the ring I bought her
and when I will propose
and how I will afford it
and how I will afford her
and if I can work at all
and if I can sleep with
all the dogs
and all the cats and all the
things that disrupt
my contentness
but I love her for these things
and wish that she would not
change
but that I would change
and I check my pocket
for loose change
I will need more cigarettes
tonight
and I stare at her again
and I love her so much
that my eyes start to water
and a tear falls on the book

and like a funeral

I cry for poetry and love

The Jazz Age

O how I love the peace
on the days with dark clouds
no sun
temperature a bit chilly
enough for a jacket
and a heater
slightly burning the hair
on my arms
and
I read
a book by Hemingway
or Fitzgerald
something olde
something classy
something about
writers speaking with writers
and wearing suits
and drinking cocktails
and smoking cigarettes
and the women
watch them speak
of art in awe
and a few even understand
and on these days I
trade my beer
for coffee or even
hot chocolate
and I read
and I read
and I think of love
and act it out
in my head
and I think not
of my appearance
of my money
of my schedule
and think only of
this world
that I so long
to live in

sunday morning poems

there's a coffee mug
half full
on my left
my ashtray
to my right
and center
is my notebook
and pen

I write some sunday morning
poems
and call my wife over
"hey, babe,
what do you think?"
and she
doesn't give an answer
she just makes
sarcastic jokes
like
"what does this mean,
poet?"
and
"is this about you
being homosexual?"

later
the mail comes
and the magazine writes
and says
"thank you
for sending us
your poems,
but they do not fit
our style."

my wife reads the letter
and says
"they are stupid.
I don't understand
how your stuff doesn't sell."

I've learned
that
she thinks
I am a good artist

she just says it
in her own
poetic way

The Burden of the Mind

F. Scott Fitzgerald wrote,
"The natural state of
the sentient adult
is a qualified unhappiness."

He's right.
I weigh three times
my body weight.

salt.

1:30 am
and I am sleeping
on the couch
and my phone is at
17% and my charger
is locked in the bedroom
with you
and I try
to squeeze in a poem -
or suicide note -

and all the cats
are screaming
and all the rabbits
are thumping
and all my temples
are pounding
and you locked the door

and I set an ant on fire
and I pour salt on wounds
and I turn the handle again

and you locked the door

Postcard from North Adams, MA

I've envied travelers
experiencing all
the tastes
the smells
the sights

they gave you
maturity
intelligence
empathy

after 22 years
I traveled alone
and tasted
and smelled
and saw

and I don't want to
do it again
not
without you

I cried in
the car
the airplane
the bars

I ate at the restaurants
by pretending
you were across from me
or else
my food would
get cold

I thought my
life
and
death
was dictated
by
how much freedom I had

but
you are my freedom

I still want(need)
to travel

quite often

but
cliche-ly
ONLY WITH YOU

sincerely
R. Masso

Return Postcard from North Adams, MA

I always thought
you were more
independent
than me

there was
never
any doubt
in my mind
that you would
be fine
by yourself

we are together
constantly
and
maybe we need
to practice being
apart
for other times
when you travel

go play
make music
wake up early and explore
and make me some art

draw me a rhino

sincerely

Petting Zoo on Lower Landing Rd

at 10:15 I am in bed

at 10:20 the cat climbs on me
at 10:48 the ferrets start wrestling
at 11:11 the rats drink for three minutes
at 11:33 the cat spills yesterday's coffee
at 12:54 the rabbit starts thumping
at 1:26 the cat throws up
at 2:17 the chinchilla jumps in his cage
at 2:39 the ferrets drink for two minutes
at 3:44 the rats fight
at 4:15 the rabbit drinks for one minute
at 4:49 the cat hisses at the ferrets

at 5:30 I go to work

Oh, Artie!

another bar,
this time in Berlin,
and on dark beer number 3
an elderly American couple
sits down next to me
and smiles
at my tattooed body
and I smile back
and the wife says,
"Oh, Artie! Look at these
cocktails! Which one should
I try?"
"This one, sweetheart."
he replied
and orders himself
whiskey on the rocks
and some appetizers
and I order another beer
and a sandwich -
I am not hungry, but
I want to witness this couple -
and the wife shrieks
"This cocktail is just wonderful!
Try it, try it, Artie!"
and then I hear
"Oh, Artie! What great
zucchini fries! Look at the
presentation!"
and I continue to smile
while finishing a few
more beers
and my sandwich
and I listen and look
at their love
that has stood the test
of time
and I am reminded
that life is impressive
and taste is a gift
and sight is a blessing
and art is everywhere

and every plant is different
and every sip is different
and every bar is different

and when they get up
to leave
I thank them
and they ask what for
and I say

the buzz.

one for two

I do nothing
in poetry,
not art,
without meaning

each line is under another
next to another
split for a reason

each word is under another
next to another
lowercase for a reason

it is a form of painting
visual as much as
verbal
and a word spaced
barely to
the left
      or
            under
or   ALonE
can change
the enjoyment
or meaning
for the reader
   and writer

even when I post
these poems
on   INSTAGRAM (in 2018)
they are black text
      white background
times new roman
11pt font   like
an application for
a job interview
- which I infer this is

I beg the reader

to view my work
as well thought out and
artistic -
at least visually

because the same
cannot always be said
for the
       words.

Note to Self

I've learned
that if I write
while I'm
upset
depressed
angry
scared
or any other
emotion

my poems turn out
too angst-y
too childish
too bitch-y
too fake
or any other
synonym for shit

I have to journal
my immature feelings
and go back to them
when I am neutral
whatever the hell
neutral is

write drunk edit sober
only applies to being
legitimately drunk

not drunk on emotion

I must write about feeling
after I've felt it
instead of being in the
eye of the hurricane
or else
I sound like a teenager

and no one likes teenagers

the herd

it was a tuesday
at 5:45 pm
and I saw an opening

it was two lanes to my right
and I was boxed in
by a ford in front of me
by a toyota to the right of me

I couldn't get to it

I saw a car
zoom in between lanes
at 85 mph
and I saw him
get into the opening
and he zoomed even faster
and he zoomed
until he was gone
and I felt like applauding
and I felt like shouting
and I was filled
with happiness

at least one of us
broke free

non-refundable

in bed earlier than usual
never a good sign
and there is a cat on me
and another cat drinking
and she is tired of traveling
so she lays away from me
and she hears me typing
and gives a dirty look
and I try to type quieter
but she gets up
and goes into another room
and I am alone
and my head hurts

and the flight is non-refundable

Mr. Knuckles

my bills are due
and the company is closing
and I need to get her a ring
and get us a house
and feed the dogs
and feed the cats
and my taste is that
of the celebrity that
I am not
yet

and I drive past a man
with his head sideways
and a puke-stained shirt
and a face made from
the knuckles of bar patrons
and he is talking to himself
as he walks to
wherever he wants
next

and I wonder
if it would be easier
to be an alcoholic

Lumos

a four-month old kitten
with wedding white
fur
and cobalt-Cobain eyes
was found on the pike
and given to my girlfriend
and I -
we(she) had a lot of animals
(he made 26)
and she acquired most this way -

and he was a
fireball
and a
fighter
and would
climb up our pants
and our necks
and jump in our bowls
still filled with food

and then one day
I found him
barely able to breathe
with pale gums
and pleading eyes

so we took him to the vet
and they put him on oxygen
and drugs
and didn't reassure us
and I didn't cry
and I wanted to
and I waited

and my girlfriend called
the vet a few hours
later
and they said
he was doing much better
and he was play fighting

with the vet techs
and climbing everywhere

and I almost cried again
because he had such
a love and a zest
for life
and the world needs that
and I need that

and that four-month old
loved life
enough to not let it go
and to fight
until it was out of his control

and he was
a better man
than me

light of life, black of death

what do you do
when the alcohol is gone
and the stores and bars
are closed
and the cigarettes
make your stomach hurt
and she
won't talk to you
or lay on your bed

and you witness
the light of life
and the black of death
and you have no more tears
for a tissue
or a typewriter
or a canvas
and you look at your art
and want to burn it
and throw it away
and the only answer is sleep

but sleep got you into this
too much of it
too little of it
never waking up from it

and the sun has gone
and the moon with it
and the stars are together
holding each other
yet separate
and they mock you

and they mock you
and they mock you
and they throw you a noose
but your head doesn't fit
and you want it to
and you don't

and you beg
but you don't know what for
and you sweat
but it's not hot
and you curse
but you don't know who

what do you do
when you can't do anything

Last Will and Testicle

when I die
before you

I want you to move on
find someone new
someone who loves you
and respects you
someone to make memories with
and enjoy the rest of your days with
someone to lie with at night
and vent to
and talk to about your day
and help you financially
and I want you
to find someone to love
not as much as me
and who knows that
he will never replace me
or be loved by you
more than you loved me
but I don't want you
to be sad
or alone
I want you to be free
and happy

I know that is what I am
supposed to say

I know I am supposed
to be selfless

but if you die
before me

you would want me
to be alone
and not marry
and not love
and not fuck

you would want me
to wear your ashes
like a tribal tattoo

so I want the same for you

how it's supposed to be

I wish I saw every experience
good or bad
as a new experience
an experience I
wouldn't have had
otherwise
and my skin
would become stone
and sadness become
curiosity
and happiness
become unexpected
instead of
only seeing
poverty
divorce
unemployment
boredom
death
and other general
annoyances
as general annoyances

more love could be had
and
less cigarettes could be smoked

hands of a god

there's something maturing
about fixing your own tire

jacking up the car
putting your body weight
behind each turn
of the lugs
kicking the tire off
carrying the sonofabitch
to the nearest mechanic
walking in with the tire
on your shoulder
and your chest held high
like it's a trophy
smoking cigarettes as you wait
admiring the cuts and dirt
on your hands
and repeating the process
in the opposite order

you take in the world
you hear the silence
you alone

accomplishing this task
is like an awakening
of the spirit
you realize how hard
and easy life is

there's a metaphor
in changing a tire

I just don't know what it is

Ding, Ding, Ding

she's late
  getting home again
and I sit
and I have no beer
and my mind
is a bird
under a silver dinner dome
and I look at a black cat
and I look at a grey cat
and I look at a brown cat
and I look at a white dog
and I look at a black dog
and I look at a brown dog
and I imagine them older
and then dying
and I try to decide
if I will be around to see
these events unfold

and I get in my car
and I go
to the
liquor
store

greener

making love in a loft
nothing but glass
so the world can watch

making love while
the city eats and shits
and drinks and sweats

making love while
they drive to appointments
and drive to funerals

making love while
they work
and I do not

making love
better than ever
in a new place

nothing brings about
great love making
like traveling

but heed the warning

it will end when you
go back home

inspiration without adaptation

your poems
look just like
bukowski

you talk
too much about
hunter s. thompson

you are
going to die like
hemingway

you have
no voice like
leonard cohen

you need to stop
writing about the age of
fitzgerald

I am not
being anyone but
masso

I understand
your confusion though

finding
inspiration without adaptation
is a hard thing to accomplish

death of a salesman

i know
i know
i do not know
i know
nothing everything
you me him
her
this beer
        this cigarette
     this pornography
   this money i am
spending
to forget
   to remember
you me
them
her
                       it

i love it
i love this
i love all this
yet i curse you
    for your emotions
  cause they affect
        mine
and make me
do this love this
love you
love you dearly
love you truly
love you love me
please love me
please don't forget me
       don't forget me

come to bed
i promise
         promise?

come to bed

brachium

her arm
is around me
as I lay on my back
and type this
as quietly as I can
so that I don't wake her
and

my arm
is under her
head as she sleeps
and I look at her face
her precious face
and see her innocence
and my lack of
and I worship her
for she knows
of my past
and my sins
and my love
and she has no sins
and if she did
I would not love
me her me her
as she loves
me her me her
and
a shooting star
just flew by the window
and I wish a selfish wish
and I kiss her forehead
and she inches closer to me
and

our arms
overlap
and I adore her
and my wish has come true
and
I
close the type

writer

both

a virus and a parasite
walk into a bar

the virus orders a beer
the parasite orders gin
I drink both

while my wife gently sleeps

better than you

ah yes
indeed
quite extraordinary
what do you think of the wine?
more brandy, dear?
your poetry is superb
as is your business
likewise to your politics
and a toast to your music
caviar
and wellington
compliments of the chef
have some french cheese
I enjoy your fashion
only the best for us, darlings

I go home
take my pants off
open a beer
scratch my balls
shit
burp
and snore

ballet

I got yelled at
for buying a chair
because I am
out of work again
"but that is what
credit cards are for",
I said,
"and I needed a chair"
and she told me to get a job
one that can buy a bigger house
and more dinners
cooked by the best
and more clothes that
the one percent wear
and I stared forward
and told her that there
are no careers left
and even if there were
that I don't want them
and that I would be wasted
on them
and she left
and slammed the door
and I sipped my beer
and continued watching
professional wrestling -
two sweaty guys
in a ballet of art and emotion -
and they are not being
wasted by performing

and then I wrote this poem
and I once again
worked for free

Inner Child

I thought
at some point
you became an
adult

I thought at
eighteen
you became confident
        mature
          happy

a forty-eight year old
told me
as he counted his money
that happiness
and confidence
comes and goes
like the wave
drowning a
surfer

the adult told me
as he looked at his feet
that he still feels small
           anxious
            naive
in front of other adults

I took a drag
of my cigarette
and looked
at the clouds
go by

our inner child
knows
no age

a spider

I was writing a different poem
but I have stopped
and now I am writing this one
because ten feet
away
from me
there is a spider
climbing up the wall

I do not know
why they paralyze me
with such fear

I keep looking up at him
after every word
making sure he keeps
his distance

he has turned
and is staring at me

I wonder who is more afraid

does he know
that he is winning?

size means nothing
like an ocean
in space

I fantasize about killing him
but cannot seem to move

he finally finds a crack
and leaves my sight

I sip my coffee
and light another cigarette

where did I put my other poem?

60 Degrees

it has been a much
too dead stop
     winter
but today
I am outside
with my typewriter
with my cigar
with my t-shirt
with my beer
and I am watching
the dogs run around
the yard
panting
and barking
and happy

and I haven't sent
a single publisher
anything this
whole winter
and today that will change
and my pockets
will feel heavier
and I will get
a summer body
and a broken
fall

and spring can go
fuck itself

and I think that
life is beautiful
but I think it
with caution
for tomorrow
I have to work
and I will
once again
pray for the
snow

a book you still hide

a story,
a story,
tell me a story!

a fox and a cat
a moth and a fire
a bear eats my arm
a hitman for hire

a life surely wasted
a rat in my trap
a balloon up too high
a line on your map

a song that you sing
a gun in the dark
a plane coming down
a love without spark

a gift to the homeless
a present for me
a shallow wet pool
a fear you can see

a new way to die
a hill full of pride
a zoo without you
a book you still hide

a god in the sky
a pole in the ground
a juggler and mime
a herd without sound

a thief in the night
a room smells of grape
a vase shatters now
a black cassette tape

a steel bar in front
a grown man is crying

a pastor spills ink
a lion is dying

Power

He had too much empathy,
and not enough power,
to play God with others,
so he played God on himself.

4am

there's a routine
every morning at 4am:

she leaves,

I take a drink,
I masturbate,
I close my eyes,
I do not sleep,
I tap one foot against
the other foot as fast as
I can,
I get up,

I wait.

#002

maybe i shouldn't complain so much. i have quite a nice life, after all. maybe not measured in millions, but maybe i should not be a hypocrite. i speak greatly of the evils of caring about money, yet it fuels my depression more so than anything else. I seek a life of societal separation, of self sustainability, yet, when i am not in the woods i seek the best food, the best items, the best house, even the best resources for the outdoors - the best rods, the best hiking boots, the best hammock, the best jacket. what's the fun in that? using the best money can buy let's you get by with less knowledge. i like learning and challenging myself, but want the easiest job. i live in a creek of contradiction and i keep thinking i have to pick a side. but why? as long as the creek dries up, i can camp in the middle. absolute freedom is ridding labels. instinct driven. gratitude. come whatever may. shut up, fuck face.

1,715 ft.

the peace
washes over me
like
an isolation tank
like an airport beer

when driving
for hours
past trees
and mountains
and plains

to hike
far far away
far far away

so high
that my boss
can't find me

so high
that the debt collectors
can't see me

so high
that the others
can't hear me

the peace
washes over me
like
an imperfect song
like an acoustic guitar

when I park
at the base
and start to ascend
and reach
the top

so high

that my phone
can't survive
when I throw it
off the cliff
1,715 ft

the peace
washes over me
like
an easy friday
like an old monk

when I sit
at the top
for hours
and hours
and find home

in me
and this world

the peace
leaves me
when I start
to descend
and re-enter
the workforce

the peace
is gone
when I buy
a new phone

16th and Locust

you get numb

to
the fights
the beatings
the needles in arms
the sniffing
the vomit under your seat
on the train

you get numb

so
you don't call the cops
you keep walking forward
you don't make eye contact
you keep your head down
you lift your legs
and continue riding

keep reading your paperback
and
keep your feet up

you
will get home
eventually

I

you don't deserve to be
            downstairs

I fucked up,
I should be

you do everything
I ever want
and
I constantly make you regret
it and you
still constantly do it

you're absolutely perfect
and
I know you don't think your anxiety
at our wedding
was because of marrying me,
but I did,
and I do,
and even in the moment,
I never blamed you for it -
I expected it,
prepared myself to be
stood up at the alter
weeks before -
I thought you'd come
to your senses,
or at least say
"push it back until you're worthy
of being married"

I was really good
at being
an early twenties artist
with a zest for life
and
I was good at being a guide
for you to
become who you are

the problem is
I never grew up
I never kept a job
without a vice

I was in shape as a wrestler,
but had no money
fat as a musician,
but had no money
and
now I have money,
and a career,
and a wife,
and
I'm an alcoholic
to deal with having a life
that is for an adult
and
not a child

actually,
I was an alcoholic
when I was young,
too,
just not the kind I am now

I kept you up on first dates,
and second dates,
and 365th dates
until 2am
when you had work at
5am
every single night/day
at bars or
with beers on my porch

I know this
I know all of this

you married the boy
I was
hoping he'd become a man

but now I'm this

a narcissist alcoholic
who will only be happy
with complete freedom,
never compromising,
who needs no job
so he can workout
and
eat right on your dime,
and hide behind nothing -
but all of his friends are alcoholics,
and his career is
making the product he hides behind,
and the solution is to start over again…

like he's an early twenties artist.

no money,
no job,
no friends

just like you found me
just like you found me

but now we have a house,
and a family,
and I have to work tomorrow,
and I have to be an adult now,
because I have no more chances,
so that year,
or three years,
or seven years of rehab,
and finding friends
and building another career -
those numbers can't be,
they don't have the time to exist

I'm no longer the boy
I'll never be the man
I'm not just like you found me

all I am,

is terrified to lose you,
but terrified to change

3/26/22

i am an alcoholic. mission accomplished. i am in the shower needing to shit another beer shit, masturbating for the fourth time before noon, and keeping my family waiting on me - waiting to go out drinking with them. no clean laundry for the fifth week in a row. no chores done around the house. dogs are skinny and depressed. every animal has gotten an ass beating from me lately. i hate myself and want to die. it's been over two years of this now. well, since i was 20 probably, but worse than ever the last two years. i have a memory of my dad calling me a quitter and not as tough as my brother that my therapist won't let me process yet until i stop drinking, but i'm drinking because of it. and i have a career now as a brewer. i have to change every part of my life, or be a functioning alcoholic forever. we haven't fucked in over two weeks. she hasn't kissed me in just as long. she is now above me. i see no reason to quit my career and friends. i'd be lost without that, and lost without her. i need both. Taylor Hawkins died.

Scottsville, Virginia

I had to go
to a small town
in Virginia
for a book signing

the town had a population
of twenty

me
my wife
seventeen soulless poets
and one person with everyone's book
but mine

we tried to find
activities
or
alcohol
to hold us over
for our stay
but
only found
our hotel bed
night after night

after listening to
metaphors
about the sun
and moon
and happiness
for three days
we were finally allowed to leave

we went into a gas station
on our drive home
for cigarettes
and the toilet
and there was horse racing
on a tv
and someone came in
and placed a bet

he then joined
the seventeen people
staring at the tv

I went to the counter
and asked for cigarettes
and decided to place a bet

I left
after I was handed my cigarettes
deciding that it didn't matter
if I won

but I bought a ticket anyway

I needed to do something
stupid
in that town

I needed to get
the adrenaline flowing,
to be a degenerate or rebel
for just one second

I never did
check which horse
came out on top

maybe
I'm a millionaire

I'm happy
not knowing

Born too late

A publisher wrote back to me
"Your work is too Bukowski.
I don't like Bukowski."

What he wanted to write was
"Your work won't sell.
I need money."

Maybe he's right.
Maybe it won't sell,
but at least it has soul.

I wrote back
"I understand.
Thanks for reading."

What I wanted to write was
"You make soulless poets rich.
Good writing isn't just metaphors."

I may sound like Bukowski,
but I'm not faking my art,

he was just born first.

24 hours

how is a man supposed to

paint
write
read
send publishers art
take photographs
smoke cigars
drink beer
travel somewhere new
make love
spend time with his wife
walk the dogs
pet his cats
clean the pets cages
watch documentaries
be in a band
exercise
maintain friendships
go to school
go to work
and
sleep

all in one day?

maybe the problem isn't
how fast we revolve
around the sun

maybe I just have too many
                       hobbies.

a conversation on a park bench

"Do you ever wish
you fucked your mom?"
he asked.

"No." I said
and continued staring
at the pigeons
he was feeding.

He was homeless
      dirty
        drunk
but I gave him a few sips
of my
brown paper bag
anyway

his conversation interested me.

"Never?" he said
"I'm not weird for thinking that,
right?
Freud said it was normal!"

"I guess" I said
"Isn't it a little early in the day
to talk like this?"

"You're drunk, right?"

"True."

"I can't figure out what it is
but I have this desire
like a longing
    an emptiness
to fuck her.
You don't have that?"

I watched him continue
throwing bread on the ground.

"Why are you throwing food
to birds
when you are homeless
and starving?"

He looked at me.

"It's moldy.
I have standards."

full-time

I apologize
for being unapologetic
and I wish
that wasn't the case
but
I am
because I have yet
to get paid

and you see me
as only a busboy
or a poor stocker
and minimum wage
worker

there is no
validation
for being
a creep
or weirdo
or murderer
or pedophile
or harsh
or blunt
or a thief

if only I sold more books
or lived in a bigger house
or drove a luxury car

then I would
be allowed
to be
myself

Hemingway's Challenge Pt.2

She has a home but no house to surround it.

Hemingway's Challenge Pt.5

I use(d) to be able to deal with life.

watching the game at a brewery

there is something about
a beer
sitting on a wooden table

the table can be glossy
or not

it could be sitting
in a park
or parking lot
or warehouse
or mansion
or cemetery
or amongst other
wooden tables
with beers upon them

but that is your table
       your beer

and it's worth

your paycheck
and
your stress
and
your self

there is something about
. ….
……. .. . …… …..

and in the repeating
words of
Dickinson

"a gentile metaphor
that is full of
shit"

"K"

The clouds swayed out of the way,
attaching themselves to the sides of the looking-glass,
to reveal the green of your eyes -
the same green as your dress.

You were surrounded by a maze
of rose bushes, while
standing under a sign
with your name written on it.

The "K" from the wrought-iron sign fell
and it made the most beautiful sound,
a "ting", but also a "bang"
as it cracked the concrete.

An elf, dressed like a conductor,
blue pinstripes on top of white,
rode a tiny train to the fallen "K"
and placed a bell over it.

The elf gave you a rubber hammer
and you hit the bell.

You grabbed my hand
and led me through the maze.

new york,
    new york

a weird looking word
a weird looking spelling
a weird looking life

get on train
get off train

walk to bagel shop
one of a thousand

get bagel
one of a thousand

with lox
one of a thousand

walk to mini
disneyland-esque stores

spend money
on things I will never display

meet someone
more famous than you

one of a thousand
living larger than you

one of a thousand
living better than you

walk past hot dog stands
one of a thousand

get a hot dog
one of a thousand

go to an irish pub
one of a thousand

drink a guiness
one of a thousand

get on train
get off train

no one cared
no one judged me

unlike philly
I was one of a thousand

evolution: 1

I don't want to
leave this cabin
or
go back to work
or
go back to rent
or
go back to life

I want to
cut wood for fires
and
live where we all know
each other -
happy hour hangouts
and
cornhole by the
O'Flaherty's RV
every Tuesday
and Thursday night

guys pound beers
and spit tobacco
and girls
drink cocktails
from a can
watching on

and when you need
something
anything
the one store has it
with the same worker
and the same prices

and the woods
and the rivers
and the cabins
and the fires
and the stars
and the days

and the nights
and the freedom

and I don't want
to go back

I will be miserable
going back

and Darwin
is smarter
than god

glee

i was so happy
    two days ago

and thought i
and   life
were doing just fine

but
she is sleeping
in a separate room a-
              gain

because i am
a child
so i figured i should
journal/write
instead of
watch a doc on death/
listen to Keaton Henson
like
an adult

but
i am
neither child nor
         adult
i am Cory Monteith?
i am all three curses?

i am tired.

here is your journal

time to be an adult
and masturbate,
not sleep,
and not work tomorrow

My Masterpiece

my funeral will be my last
                         artistic masterpiece
watch what I can make you feel

Acknowledgements

"Home"
"My Masterpiece"
"Power"
were first published by *Spillwords Press*.

"at the airport"
"Bukowski"
were first published by *Duane's PoeTree*

cover art by robbie masso
back photograph by stephanie callaghan

www.ingramcontent.com/pod-product-compliance
Lightning Source LLC
Chambersburg PA
CBHW070757020526
44118CB00036B/1852